AMISTAD RISING

A STORY OF FREEDOM

VERONICA CHAMBERS

Illustrated by PAUL LEE

HARCOURT BRACE & COMPANY

San Diego   New York   London

For Marcus John and Andrea Polans,
for blessing me with their amistad
— V. C.

For Wendy
— P. L.

Library of Congress Cataloging-in-Publication Data
Chambers, Veronica.
Amistad rising: a story of freedom/by Veronica Chambers; illustrated by Paul Lee.
p. cm.
Summary: A fictional account of the 1839 revolt of Africans aboard the slave ship *Amistad*
and the subsequent legal case argued before the Supreme Court in 1841 by
former president John Quincy Adams.
ISBN 0-15-201803-4
I. Amistad (Schooner)—Juvenile fiction. [I. Amistad (Schooner)—Fiction.] I. Lee, Paul C., ill. II. Title.
PZ7.C3575Am 1998
[Fic]—dc21 97-27987

First edition
A C E F D B
Printed in Mexico

The illustrations in this book were done in acrylic on Bristol board.
The display type was hand-lettered by Tom Seibert.
The text type was set in Centaur.
Color separations were made by Bright Arts, Ltd., Hong Kong.
Printed and bound by RR Donnelley & Sons, Reynosa, Mexico
This book was printed on totally chlorine-free Nymolla Matte Art paper.
Production supervision by Stanley Redfern and Pascha Gerlinger
Designed by Lisa Peters

Amistad Rising: A Story of Freedom
is based on the true story of Joseph Cinqué. Most of the
book is factual, though we've imagined Cinqué's words and feelings and
some of his actions in order to bring life to a journey that
happened more than 150 years ago. —V. C. and P. L.

Many thanks to the authors of and contributors to
the following sources:

Jones, Howard. *Mutiny on the Amistad*. Oxford University Press, 1987.

Martin, Edmon B. *All We Want Is Make Us Free: La Amistad and the
Reform Abolitionists*. University Press of America, 1986.

Owens, William A. *Slave Mutiny: The Revolt on the Schooner Amistad*.
J. Day Company, 1953.

The Amistad Revolt: All We Want Is Make Us Free. Audiovisual by the
Amistad Committee, Inc., 1995.

STAND HERE WITH ME on the shores of New London, Connecticut. Feel the cool breeze of the Atlantic Ocean on your face. Feel the dirt beneath your feet; this land is far from ordinary. It was here, upon this very spot, that Joseph Cinqué set foot in America, bringing with him a group of renegade slaves and leaving his mark on history.

This is a story about the changing winds of fortune, about a man who was born free, was made a slave, and battled nations to be free again. It is a true story. And like so many stories, it begins not on land but at sea.

Have you ever wondered why the ocean is so wide? It's because it holds so much history. There's not a drop of seawater that doesn't have a secret; not a river or a lake that doesn't whisper someone's name. Ask the ocean about the legend of Joseph Cinqué, and this is what you might hear.

THE YEAR WAS 1839. Owning slaves was still legal, although the stealing of slaves from Africa was not. Slavery was a huge business. Many slave traders had grown rich from selling human beings, and they were reluctant to give it up.

It was nightfall when the slave ship *Teçora* set sail from Sierra Leone, a small country on the coast of West Africa. The water rippled like quicksilver in the moonlight as the ship voyaged toward Cuba. But in the ship's hold, more than five hundred Africans were held prisoner. There was no toilet, there was no bath, and the stench was unbearable. The Africans were chained together in pairs. Heavy iron shackles bound their hands and their feet. Movement was difficult. Escape was impossible. Disease and malnutrition claimed the lives of many; others perished under the murderous beatings of the slave traders. The dead were tossed overboard without a thought.

After two tempestuous months at sea, the *Teçora* arrived in Cuba. There, fifty-three of the prisoners — including four children — were sold to two Spanish slave traders and forced to board yet another ship to take them to a Cuban plantation.

This ship was called *Amistad*, the Spanish word for "friendship."

Three days into the journey, the *Amistad* sailed through an unexpected storm. The ship was battered by roaring rain and wind. The trip took longer than the crew expected and provisions were low. Each slave survived on a daily meal of two potatoes, a banana, and just a little water.

In the hold of the ship, a young man tried to quell his unsettled stomach. Fear gripped him as he watched his fellow Africans suffer and starve. He was young and afraid, but destiny had a plan for him. His name was Singbe, although the slavers had given him the Spanish name Joseph Cinqué, and he belonged to a group of people called Mende who lived near Sierra Leone. He had been working on a village road when he was seized and sold to the slavers of the *Teçora*.

During the first two months of his captivity, Cinqué was disturbed to find that he had begun to forget little things about Africa—the smell of freshly harvested rice, the color of the sunsets, the feel of wet grass beneath his running feet. When he closed his eyes, he could see these things only as distant and blurry as a dream. But he could never forget the people he had left behind. His wife. His three children. His mother and father.

Every day Cinqué grew more restless, wondering what the Spaniards intended to do with him and the other Africans. Though they were forbidden to speak, his companions whispered questions: What lay ahead? What would slavery mean? Would they simply be transported from ship to ship indefinitely?

Cinqué had to find out.

Occasionally, a few captives were allowed on deck for some air. Cinqué waited for his turn, and when he was finally ushered above, he attempted to coax some answers from Celestino, the cook. The two men communicated with hand gestures, for neither spoke the other's language.

Cinqué demanded to know what would happen to them.

Celestino smiled devilishly, intent on playing a cruel joke. He pointed to barrels of beef and signaled to Cinqué that the slave traders planned to kill the Africans, cut them up, salt them for preservation, and eat them like cured beef.

Fear and anger filled Cinqué. He would not be eaten by the white men who held him captive. He would not.

He decided to strike that night. With a loose nail he had found earlier in a deck board, he picked the lock on his shackles, freeing himself and then the other prisoners. Once free, they quieted the four children and searched the cargo hold. A box of sugarcane knives was discovered — a boon!

Sneaking up to the deck, they took the crew by surprise. In the fight, Celestino, the captain, and one African were killed. Two of the crew jumped overboard. Three were taken prisoner. Cinqué needed them to navigate the ship back toward Africa, back toward home. When the sun rose again, Cinqué and his companions greeted the day as free people.

But they had claimed victory too soon.

Cinqué ordered the Spaniards to steer the ship toward the rising sun. They obeyed and sailed the ship east toward Africa during the day, but then at night turned the ship around and sailed northwest toward North America. For two months the ship pitched back and forth across the Atlantic Ocean. Nine more Africans died during that time — some from their battle wounds, some from food poisoning, and some from starvation.

Then, on August 27, 1839, the *Amistad* was escorted by an American ship into the harbor of New London, Connecticut. Weary, hungry, and hopelessly lost, Cinqué and the others were forced to come ashore.

An American naval lieutenant saw the possibility for quick profits in the Africans. But this was the North, and a group of whites and free blacks campaigning against the institution of slavery was gaining popularity. They called themselves abolitionists, and they took on Cinqué and the other Africans as their most important case.

The Africans were sent to prison in New Haven, Connecticut, until a decision could be made.

The abolitionists managed to find a translator, and Cinqué told his story in a U.S. court. He was only twenty-five years old, but his experience on the *Amistad* had given him the confidence of a much older man.

The courtroom was crowded, and many were moved by Cinqué's impassioned words.

"I am not here to argue the case against slavery," Cinqué said, "though I will say it is a sin against man and God. I am here to argue the facts. The indisputable, international law is that the stealing of slaves from Africa is now illegal."

"The men who kidnapped us, who beat and tortured us, were—and are—guilty of this crime," Cinqué continued.

"We are a peaceful people. We regret the loss of life caused by our mutiny. But we are not savages. We took over the ship to save our lives. We have done no wrong. Allow us to go home."

The weekend before the judge made his decision, Cinqué and his companions waited in the New Haven jail, their hearts filled with fear and hope. The judge held the power to make the Africans slaves or to set them free. On Monday morning, January 13, 1840, they worried no longer. He had decided they should be returned home.

They were free.

But as Cinqué was soon to learn, the passage to freedom was as winding as the *Amistad*'s journey across the sea. President Martin Van Buren, concerned that freeing the Mende would enrage southern slave holders, ordered the district attorney to file an appeal so the case would be heard in the U.S. Supreme Court. And because of this, Cinqué gained his greatest American ally: former president John Quincy Adams.

Having heard about the mutineers, Adams came out of retirement to argue Cinqué's case. He was seventy-two years old. It had been more than thirty years since he had argued a case in a courtroom, and the thought of bearing the responsibility for this one worried the elderly statesman deeply.

But inspired by Cinqué, whom many of the abolitionists had begun to refer to as the Black Prince, Adams tirelessly prepared his defense. In court he spoke on behalf of the Mende for seven and a half hours. Sweat poured from his brow, and his voice filled the packed courtroom as he presented his case. There were many factors at play: Were the Africans the rightful property of the Spaniards? Were they brutal murderers? Or were they freedom fighters, no different than the men and women who had rebelled against England and founded the United States of America? There was also international pressure. Spain wanted the slaves and the *Amistad* returned to Cuba; could the United States risk provoking European ire over the lives of the thirty-five surviving Africans?

After Adams made his closing arguments, the Supreme Court retired to deliberate. For Cinqué and the others, the fearful process of waiting and praying began again.

A week later, on March 9, 1841, the Supreme Court announced that Adams had prevailed.

The Africans were truly free.

It took eight months for the abolitionists to raise the money for the Africans' long journey back to West Africa. But at last the ship sailed, and when the African coast was finally in sight, Cinqué gathered everyone together.

"Let us give praise and thanks," Cinqué called out, his voice booming across the deck. "By the strength of our spirit and with the assistance of our ancestors, we are not slaves today. Our children will not be slaves. And their children will not be slaves. We are exactly as God willed us to be. My brothers, my sisters, we are free." Savoring the word, he let it melt like sugar on his tongue. He paused and then tasted the word again. "Free," he said, more softly now.

Each person aboard the ship felt the word coming up from their hearts, tasted the sweetness of it in their mouths, then released it into the salty sea air. "Free," they said in unison. "We are free."

IF YOU STAND right here on the New London shore, you can hear the words of the great Joseph Cinqué. His voice is so powerful that it travels across both space and time. If you bend down to the Atlantic, you can hear it in the beating of the waves. The wind whispers it as it blows around your head. And when the rain falls, it's like tears of happiness.

You can hear his words almost anywhere you
listen for them: "We are free. Free. Free. Free."